I0837947

18 STEPS

TO

WRITE

YOUR BOOK SUCCESSFULLY

How to start, develop and finish every book you write or intend to write without abandoning your book project.

IREDAFENEVESHO OWOLABI

Copyright © Iredafenevesho Owolabi 2022

Some other Fast-selling Books By the author are:

- 4-D THINKING
- How to Self-Publish Your Books Successfully
- Why you should Write a Book
- Profitable Problem Solving
- Idea to Profitable Creation
- How to Make Millions as an Author-preneur
- Kingdom Verities
- How to Enjoy Kingdom Currency (Vol. 1)
- How to Maximize Kingdom Currency (Vol. 2)
- Kingdom Currency for Students, Graduates and Businessmen (Vol. 3)
- Unlocking Your Kingdom Creativity
- 15 Hot Markets Where You Can Easily Sell Your Book Anytime
- 10 Ways to Make Money from a Single Book Idea

To Contact the author for feedbacks, to share or tell a story perhaps for inclusion in one of the future books by the author or to schedule him for a presentation, kindly send a mail to _writeyourbook@iredafeowolabi.net_ **or** _iredafeowolabi@gmail.com_.

About Me

Hi, my name is Iredafenevesho Owolabi (or Dafe for short). I help busy moms, dads, business owners and professionals write and launch their first or next book in 30-60 days or less.

I am a busy Dad, an Author of 16+ books, a professional Software Engineer based in Canada, and the world is my oyster. I facilitate seminars, trainings, workshops and conferences for individuals and groups of different kinds.

My books are being read in different parts of the world with countless testimonials of their impact. From my experience and results as a self-published author of 16 books comprising more than 10 books in hard copies, soft copies, audio version, and many different formats, I have learned the tricks of the writing and self-publishing trade.

I hope you do find value out of this book. If at any point you would like to pick my brain, work with me or you need me to handhold you as you embark on your first or next book project, feel free to shoot me an email at iredafeowolabi@gmail.com, or writeyourbook@iredafeowolabi.net. You can also send me a DM on Instagram or Facebook via handle @iredafeowolabi, and we can go from there. Do have a good read!

INTRODUCTION

As I sat in my home office one hot summer evening, punching the keys of my laptop, while developing a chapter for my 17th book, something sensational hit me. I saw with the eyes of my mind, a lot of people out there who have not been able to start, develop or complete at least one of the books they could potentially deliver to their world. I was awakened to a sense of urgency to help you. The mere thought of the many people out there who are pregnant with great books that may never be written triggered within me a yearning. That was when it dawned on me without equivocation that it was time to give back and help someone like you to at the very least, start, develop, and finish your first or next book.

After witnessing the birth of my first daughter, I asked myself, "What would make a woman go through all this pain and discomfort to conceive and birth a child"? I got my answer inwardly, "it is the joy of seeing the baby she carried for 9 months come into the world". Having an idea to write a book can be likened to a woman getting pregnant for a baby and successfully giving birth. It is a thing of joy when that woman finally delivers her baby and everyone can see, smell, hear and touch the baby – what started as an idea. That is what it means to birth your brainchild in form of a book! As an author of 16 books and counting, I know what the challenges of writing a book can be like. However, the joy that ensues when you hold a copy of your book or get feedback about how people loved your book or enjoyed reading it makes it worth the while. As a matter of fact, the birth pains you go through in a bid to birth your brainchild in form of a book is nothing to be compared with the fulfillment that comes with writing and publishing your book. It is that joy I want you to have by showing you the steps to write your books successfully through this piece of writing.

Everybody has the potential to write a book because everyone has a story to tell or some knowledge, experience, skill and expertise to share at different stages of their life's journey. However, even though there is a book inside of everyone, not everyone gets to flesh out their knowledge and put it in a book because it requires regular doses of dedication, consistency, and commitment.

I have seen the inexplicable joy that comes with having a baby and the fulfilment that comes with slapping your name on a book as an author. It does not only bring you money from multiple income streams, or help you build your brand, build your authority, or launch your speaking career, it brings fulfilment and a sense of true accomplishment. This satisfaction is what I long to see you experience now that our paths have crossed, along with the fame, wealth, influence, and fortune that goes with writing your book.

And this satisfaction and fulfilment is what you will have if you take every piece of insight in this book with utmost attention.

Having witnessed the conception, development, and birth of my own baby on one hand, and the birth of 16+ books on the other hand, I can easily say that there are similarities between the feeling you get when you birth your brainchild in form of a book and when you give birth to a child. You would agree with me that not everyone who conceives seed would successfully end up with a baby in hand for several reasons. And sadly, not every potential author who is pregnant with brainchildren would go on to write a book. There are so many people walking around pregnant with great books that may never be written. This is so because some abort their brainchildren from the womb of their mind, due to discouragement, ignorance, or fear of the unknown. Some potential authors get a book idea, are excited about it, but due to lack of understanding of the necessary steps they should take, abandon the project after starting the journey. Some others allow their book brainchild die prematurely while still in the womb of their minds due to miscarriage. They lose the consistency, enthusiasm and drive that would have seen them through to the end of their book project. While some authors manage to carry their brainchildren to full term but need some extra support to finally deliver or push out their book idea in form of bankable solutions and tangible products. If you fall into any of these categories or want to avoid ever finding yourself trapped in these situations, this book is for you! It would therefore be in your best interest to read to the end.

The books that finally make it into the world are those whose author followed the steps, trusted the process, and stayed the course till they carried that book from idea to finished product. The purpose of this book therefore is simple: to give you a clear understanding of the steps involved in writing your book.

I look forward to seeing you flourish with that book idea of yours as you go through the simple and straightforward steps in this guide. See you on the other side!

STEP 1

FIND A PROBLEM, GET A SOLUTION:

It is no longer news that of all aspiring authors who venture into a writing project, only 3% end up completing it. One of the reasons many writers start and cannot complete their book is that they have no clear objective in mind. Sometimes, their book idea appears to be improperly chosen or not well tailored to fix a specific problem. If you're unclear about the reason behind your book, it would be extremely difficult to complete the project. You would be clueless as to what to write and may never put pen to paper. There is a difference between having a writer's block halfway into your writing project and abandoning your book project. As a matter of fact, writer's block can easily be taken care of when you are clear on the problem you are trying to solve with your book idea. Having a main idea to focus on per time is vital to being productive every time you sit down to write. It would be very easy to go off course and lose direction if you are constantly spinning in circles without having a specific problem your book idea is going to solve. So, before you start writing your book, ask yourself, "What need, or desperate craving is this book going to satisfy?" What question is it meant to answer or which problem is it meant to solve? What value would my book idea add to my readers? How would I translate my knowledge into words that others can read, understand, and appreciate? After getting this clear, you must make every effort to tailor your work in this direction.

STEP 2

FIND A MARKET BEFORE WRITING

To succeed in your book project, it is very important that you find a market for your product even before it is created. What most authors do is that they write about anything that comes up in their heads and publish it. After they have done that, they start making frantic efforts to find a market and end up frustrated. This is because they have put the cart before the horse. If you do not have a market for your book product, no matter how wonderful your content is, you would struggle to make sales, and no one would acknowledge nor celebrate your brilliance. That is why it is critical that you locate a market where your information product would be sold. Once that is in place, then you can go ahead and begin developing your content in a manner that is tailored for your target audience - the market.

I have come across some authors who sought my counsel on how to market and sell their books to a particular niche market. When I went through the book they had developed, I discovered that it was not really tailored to reach out to the said target market but another niche entirely. What I normally tell such authors when I come across them is that they should redesign their books and remodel it to suit the market they want it to reach out to.

Another all-important reason you need to be very certain of the niche or target market you intend to reach with your product is that it would affect your pricing. I have coached several aspiring authors on this very important step and from my interactions with them I discovered something. I noticed that a lot of people do not know that a target market must be in view when setting the prices of their book alongside other factors. People will only buy your book if they perceive that the value that they stand to get from it is much more than whatever it is priced at. That is why you must be clear on your market (who your book is designed for and why you think they need to get it) before writing.

STEP 3

MAKE SURE YOUR FOUNDATION IS IN ORDER

No amount of marketing can save a terribly crafted book. Your first duty in writing a book that would make an impact on its reader and fetch you six to seven figures is to ensure your book is great, of good standard, solves the problem it was designed to solve and is properly finished. Anything short of that would endanger your brand in the long run. The main reason for this is if a product is good, it becomes easy to market it and sometimes, it markets itself. Marketing will not save you if you produce an inferior content or material. Marketing only gets potential customers to try your product, once they are not satisfied with your book, they would simply not buy any other book from you. They won't stop there, but they would go ahead to make sure other people do not make the mistake of buying from you. The bottom line is, you cannot make money or derive any benefit from writing a book if it was improperly conceived or was developed without a clear idea of who you are writing for. When you do not really know the problem that your book would help your ideal reader solve, and what exact title you should write about, your book would not yield great results. If you do not have a good product, no amount of marketing would work. It would be like putting icing on a cake that has gone bad just to attract buyers.

Even if you trick people to buy your products, no one will come back to buy from you again and that alone can de-market your brand and discourage them from repeat patronage in the future. As an author you cannot afford to put out a content that would hurt your brand. Thus, if you market an inadequate and inappropriate product, and you get some people to buy it initially, the word of mouth that would be generated from those people who were disappointed with your content would spread. Remember that bad news spreads faster than good news, therefore if that begins to happen, you will lose your repeat business opportunities and lose potential buyers. That is something you do not want to happen because the livewire of any business is in repeat patronage and positive word of mouth. That is where the money is! The best form of marketing therefore is in your ability to develop an excellent product that would leave an impact on your audience after they use them. That means you must be sure to develop a book that can "defend itself" in your absence. Once you have made up your mind to develop this kind of product, then you are good to go.

STEP 4

READ!!!

In this industry, reading and writing go together like Siamese twins. You must be a "Ben Carson" to be able to separate the Siamese twin known as reading and writing, as an author. But even Ben Carson, the renowned Neurosurgeon never attempted separating these twins (reading and writing) because he was an avid reader and a great writer himself. I know about that because I have read his books and in them, I have seen how much he reads about others and their works. Before you can become a reference point that resonates with quality, standard and value, you must have also referred to others. I have met a lot of authors who do not like to read. You do not want to listen to others, but you want to be listened to. You do not want to read other people's work, but you want people to read your work. It does not work that way. To gain command of the language you want to write in and to understand the flow and structure that works best, it is of great benefit to read works of people that interests you or tickles your fancy. Listening to audio books and podcasts could be great if you are too busy to read or reading is just not your thing. Even with these alternatives, nothing beats reading a book especially if you intend to write one that others would also read. Before I became an author, I had developed an unquenchable interest for reading books by an array of authors. I had not even conceived or entertained the idea of writing my own books, yet I would buy books and just read, read, and read! In one year, I had read 48 books just before I became a published author. If you do not buy books to read, no one would buy yours to read. This is a fact of life!

STEP 5

USE AN EYE-CATCHING TITLE AND CURIOSITY-STIRRING CAPTION

What sells a book is not so much the content as it is the title. You can have a wonderful content, yet no one would buy your book or read your book if the title is not catchy and attention grabbing enough. I bet that what first attracted you to this book you are reading right now is the title. You became interested in knowing more about the book and what it was about the moment you saw the title. The title was so compelling that you were almost sure that there was something in this book that would add value to your life and add color to your journey as an author.

There are 3 qualities a great title should have.

a. *Great titles are targeted:*

The title makes it clear exactly who the book is meant for. For example, "How to Make it Big as a Consultant" or "How to Make Millions as an Author-preneur" is a wonderful title because it tells the prospective readers exactly who the book is meant for.

b. *Great titles are result-oriented:*

The title of your book should convey the result that the potential reader can expect to get by reading it. That is why "How to Make it Big as a Consultant" is a better name than something like "Consultancy Codes". This is because the former tells the prospect what outcome they'll see after reading and applying the information given in the book while the latter doesn't. If I saw both books on a bookshelf, and I wanted to study on the subject matter, I would first choose the one that suggests to me that I would make it big or know how to make it big after reading it.

c. *Great titles are unambiguous:*

Ensure that your book title doesn't use jargons that confuse the reader and makes them think hard about what it is you have written. "How to Make Millions as a Cook" for example, leaves no question as to what the book is about or who it was designed for. It is easy to guess what the book is likely going to help the prospective reader achieve. Do not take the title of your book casually because it can either make or mar the marketing and sales process of your book. A great content would mean nothing if the title were not inviting and suggestive enough to stimulate the curiosity of potential readers.

Another very important aspect of developing your book or eBook is to craft a caption that summarizes in one sentence what your book would do for its readers. It should be a breath-taking and thought-provoking caption that sells your message at a glance. The caption is very important also because in some e-commerce sites where people buy books (e.g., Amazon) the caption of your book contributes also to the keywords that can help potential buyers locate your book. The essence of the caption is to explain further what the book can do for its readers or what it is targeted at. It could also be a simple sentence stating what the book is about in an alluring manner. When I receive a book idea and begin to conceptualize it, I write down the title in different ways and show my wife to see which one catches her attention most. That gives me a clue about what could work best as a title. You can show anyone whose judgment you trust if you do not have a spouse. Sometimes we debate on what could be a perfect title among several alternatives. She must convince me and tell me why she chooses any title she picks. I then draft as many captions as I can and try to see which one communicates the aims and objective of the book in a simple or compound sentence. Sometimes I get to modify my caption as I begin to write the book from chapter to chapter. So, keep in mind that your book title and caption are very important and requires serious thought and research to determine what it should be.

STEP 6

DO A TITLE SEARCH AND TITLE RESEARCH

Before I begin to write any book, what I do is to brainstorm a suitable title based on the previous point. I then go further to do a title search. Title search? Yes! What do I mean by a title search? I log on to Google and on Amazon and insert my proposed title into the search pane to search if there is any other book with my title. This is a very vital step if you want your book to stand out in the eyes of your potential readers on any platform when it is released. You do not want another book with the same title as yours to overshadow yours, so you need to do the search. This does not mean that if you find a book with a similar title, then you cannot use the title. However, you would do well to make sure your book stands out uniquely from the other titles on the same subject or story you intend to write on. You can achieve this by tweaking your title a bit, to avoid being overshadowed in the crowded space. This would enable you to ascertain that your title has that unique touch you want. After doing that I also search other related words to see if other authors have done a related work and I try to look up the description of such books when they pop up from an Amazon search. For example, I want to write a book about developing the mind for creativity. Let's assume the first title that came to my mind was "think different" or "think outside the box". I therefore run a search with those proposed titles. When I run the search, I could see more than ten different books by several different authors come out with the same or almost the same title as my initial title. Since I know that I need to use a uniquely different title for my book to stand out among others I try to modify my title or add a more captivating caption. I would repeat the process for different title ideas until I arrive at a unique title that stands out. I do this for every book including this one you are reading now. Do not limit yourself to Amazon and Google, the world is a global village now. You can also go on social media platforms like Instagram, Facebook, Twitter, etc., type "#yourbooktitle" on the social media search pane and see the results that come out. Having a title that other people have published on is not a bad omen, it is a good sign that there is most likely a market for what you are contemplating. You just need to make sure your title stands out and makes it clear why your book should be read instead of the others. So, if you must write a book, make sure you have something unique that differentiates your work from another author's. This step is vital to making sure that you do not get overshadowed by the competition before your book is even published. I advise you to carry out this check before you finally settle on the title of your book.

After the title search, I recommend that you begin title research to gather all relevant details and information you would like your new solution bank - book to contain. You would need to open your ears and eyes to information, conversations, read books, listen to podcasts, browse the net to see what others have said in relation to the problem you intend to solve with your book and what they have not said about it. This step is not a once-and-for-all step but one that you should do throughout the book writing process. As you do this, you are releasing your mind to fresh ideas that can make your books unique and outstanding. If there are no such materials, then ask questions to people, who are going through the problem you are trying to fix, also ask those who went through that challenge and survived it or overcame it. Just open your ears, eyes, and mind to different information outlets. It is amazing how the mind works like a magnet. The moment you set out to achieve a goal, your mind begins to attract unto you the resources, materials, information, and conversations that you need to get the insight and direction that is required to develop your project.

STEP 7

OUTLINE THE SCOPE OF WHAT YOU WANT TO WRITE BASED ON THE FOCUS AND OBJECTIVES OF THE BOOK

It would really help to have an outline of the basic thoughts and ideas you intend to share through your book. This is the part where you release your knowledge store and allow all the information you intend to write in your book to come forth. So, pick up a notepad and just dump all the information and insights you have discovered. Try to make connections between the different concepts in a way that starts from known to unknown, from cause to effect or from problem to solution.

STEP 8

BREAK IT INTO CHAPTERS

Once you have put down the basic thoughts and ideas that you want your book to contain or cover, it is time to group these different thoughts and break them into chapters. This way, you know how many chapters your book would contain and what those chapters would be about. Before I begin to write, I usually do this also and it helps me get a clear idea on how much work needs to be done for the book to be completed. As you begin writing also, this could help you break your chapters into different relevant subheadings to aid assimilation for your readers.

STEP 9

SET A TARGET AND WORK TOWARDS IT

As soon as you have your book idea well scrutinized and you have broken the idea into chapters, the next clever step to take is to set a target of how many words you want to write. You should also give yourself a timeline within which you want to accomplish this feat. That timeline should be a realistic one that you plan to work with and stick with come rain, come shine.

Whenever I start a book project and I am clear on what the book idea is about, what it should do for my readers and what each chapter title is going to be like. I always do something. I try to estimate how many words and pages would be required to communicate the message, story, experience, or expertise I intend to convey through my book. After that, I begin to project into the next few days, weeks, and months. I forecast how long it would take me to accomplish the task I have just set to achieve. I already know from experience that if my book is estimated at

60,000 words, I can begin writing and finish in 30 days if I write at least 2,000 words per day. Once I set that target, I get grinding and begin to dig the mine of my mind for treasures that should go into the book content. By doing that, I was able to write, self-publish and traditionally launch 3 books totaling about 180,000 words in 6 months. I was astounded myself when I saw the results that this principle helped me achieve. Now you do not need to write 60,000 words in a book before you can be an author. I have seen books of 5,000 to 15,000 words that end up a success. What determines how long your book should be is the content and solution you are trying to outline in the book. So, if you are serious about starting, developing, and completing your book project this principle could really help. You can also use the help of accountability partners to keep you focused and to track your progress. My accountability partner is my wife and sometimes she tracks my progress and cheers me on through the process. Just merely asking, "how was writing today?", "Did you reach your goal?" is something I have found helpful in helping me stay the course. She encourages me sometimes when I think the project may no longer be possible due to some unexpected events that distort my plans. This is one factor that helps me reach my daily writing goals. The secret to writing a book is to start right where you are. Do not let the enormity of what you need to write scare you. Do not also wait for inspiration before you start writing. As soon as you get a profitable book idea, you can start immediately. If you already have a viable book idea, just know that the best time to begin your project is now. Also know that whatever number of words you find convenient for your daily schedule, all you need to do is be consistent at reaching that target every day. That is the secret, and it works! And to reiterate what I earlier said, you do not need to write as much as 60,000 words before you can have a book. On the other hand, try not to write a pamphlet and call it a book. If you write something around the range of 30,000 words to 35,000 words for as upcoming writer, that could easily amount to 90 to 115 pages when formatted into the size of a 6×9-inch book. What matters in it all is the value that is being dished out, and not the volume of your book. In fact, I believe that less is more as we live in a world encumbered with a lot of digital distractions that steal the attention span of your average reader.

Debbie Macomber has 150 books to her name today because she was purposeful, target-oriented and she disciplined herself to put in the work. Several of her books have been named bestsellers and others adapted into movies. She has built herself more than five hundred streams of income by virtue of having 150 published books. Her generations to come would be no where next to poverty because of her works. She has received several accolades and won many awards like the Quill awards, Emmy Awards, RITA award and even a lifetime achievement award from an association of the Writers of America who specialize in her niche[1]. These trophies did not fall on her laps like ripe cherries but rather came because she made concerted efforts to birth her brainchildren and release those creations to the world. To accomplish the feat of publishing 150 books, she saw her writing as a profession, and she treated it that way. She had a business-oriented mind-set toward her craft and kept creating new products to satisfy the needs of her teeming fans and readers worldwide. Even when she had not become so wealthy from her books, she kept grinding, tilling, and digging until she struck gold with her literary works. She had a routine that helped her accomplish what appears to be an impossible feat for most authors. She gets up every morning at 4:30am, reads her Bible, and writes in her journal. At 6:00am sharp, she jumps into her swimming trunk and dives into the pool to do some laps. By 7:30am, she enters her home office and answers mails. She begins writing for the day by 10:00am every day and ends at 4:00pm[2]. She gave herself a target that helped her produce three new books a year through dedication, discipline, and perseverance.

STEP 10

WRITE PERSISTENTLY

Statistics show that out of every 100 persons who start out writing a book, only 3 eventually go on to publish them. The reason for this is that most aspiring authors lack persistence. They do not have the character and dedication to sit down and write. There are numerous factors that affect the completion of a book project. There are also many excuses that seem justifiable in the eyes of the one who is not determined. Such folks would always have reasons as to why they could not finish their book project. However, no reason is cogent enough to stop one who is persistent and determined to write, develop, and complete a book project. There is no mountain too high to climb for a man determined to write a profitable book. There is no valley too low for anyone who wants to make millions from making impact. One who wants to solve real problems with his craft, skill, ideas, and knowledge. In one of my books titled "Kingdom Currency for Students, Graduates and Businessmen", I shared a very gripping story about persistence as displayed by one of America's most profound bestselling authors of the late 1800s. It goes thus: "There was an American bestselling author named Orison Swett Marden who was born into a poor background. During his college days, he worked as a caterer and worked in hotel management. He was able to save up to $20,000 (USD) which he used as capital after his formal training. With that money he began to invest in business, was able to establish a resort and he also bought a chain of hotels in Nebraska. In 1893, there was a serious depression in the United States of America, and this affected Orison's businesses. He suffered repeated financial reversals during this depression, and he lost his hotel as a result. At the time this happened, Orison who was forty-four years of age, decided to switch career from being a businessman to becoming a professional author. Despite the serious setbacks he had suffered in business, he decided to write a book that would motivate people and inspire them to persist despite the hardship and difficulty which the nation was facing at that time. Orison therefore went on to get a little room and began to write, he spent an entire year working night and day as he wrote a book he had titled "Pushing to the Front". When he finished his manuscript one day, he decided to go out to have dinner since he was very hungry. While he was away, his room was gutted with fire and the entire manuscript was in ashes. This manuscript which was over eight hundred pages had gone up in flames and there was nothing left to recover from the fire.

Regardless of this setback, Orison out of sheer determination, persistence and diligence went to get a new notebook while his room was still in the smothering from the fire. Even though he was initially heartbroken, he picked up himself again and began to rewrite the manuscript from the memory of his dream book. After he finished rewriting the manuscript, he tried to get it into the hands of several publishers, but none was interested in a motivational book. They thought such a book would not sell as people were in challenging financial times. Unemployment was very high, and the depression seemed to be having the better part of the nation. When Orison moved to Chicago where he got another job, his friend introduced his work to a publisher friend. That was how this book "Pushing to the Front" got published and eventually became the single greatest runaway bestseller in the history of personal development books at that time. This book was so great that American politicians and presidents like William McKinley, Theodore Roosevelt, and even the Prime Minister of England, William Gladstone, praised the book. Respectable inventors and influencers like Henry Ford, Thomas Edison, Harvey Firestone and J. P. Morgan made references to this book as a major inspiration for their great accomplishments. This book would have forever been lost in the flames of the past but for his determination accompanied by the persistent and diligent effort put in by the author to make his book a dream turned reality. Orison Swett Marden went on to write fifty or more books and booklets during his career. This man said, "The world makes way for the determined man. Everybody believes in the man who persists, sticks, hangs on when others let go. Tenacity of purpose gives confidence". It takes diligence to possess the tenacity of purpose".[3]

Hear this: *Discovering a profitable book idea is not all that there is to make impact and fetch consistent income from your craft. Being tenacious in your pursuit of purpose is the only key to achieving that.* Orison Swett Marden had the best excuses, but he never used them. He could have given up after his book went up in flames and no one would have accused him of being lazy. He could have hung himself after that sad and tragic experience, but he did not let that get to him. He walked the talk and "pushed to the front" until he eventually published the book that brought to him fame and wealth untold. What is stopping you from starting, developing, and completing your first or next book? Refuse to let it hinder you or stop you. Get up and get to it! Face it squarely!

STEP 11

YOU COULD HIRE A GHOST-WRITER

This step is one that you could possibly skip but it is there nonetheless, for those who may need to take that route.

A ghost-writer gets paid to write books, articles, stories, or songs that would be credited to another person's name. This is an option that I would not recommend but I know that there are people who do not mind using this method because of their busy schedule or inability to put in the required work. If you would like to write a book but do not have the time, patience or dedication required, you can use the services of a personal assistant or a freelance ghost-writer. You can buy content from them and adapt it if it meets a need you know that people are desperate to get rid of.

President Donald Trump has his name on about 19 books as the author but almost all these books involved the work of a ghost-writer. Tony Schwartz is one of several ghost-writers Trump has used[4]. His first book "The Art of the Deal" was ghost-written by this man. Sadly, Schwarz refused to remain a ghost after writing as he seized every opportunity to tell people that Trump did not write any word of that book. That is one major disadvantage of using a ghost-writer; they could refuse to remain ghosts the moment your book becomes a runaway success.

STEP 12

RESEARCH, RESEARCH, RESEARCH

This is one of the most critical steps required to write a book that can stand the test of times. If you want your content to be durable and valuable, you must research what you write to provide first class and up to date information that can help your readers. Even when you have result based expertise, one of the best ways to help your readers grasp the principles is to give them verifiable facts and standard information. Even when you are writing a fiction or a story book, research remains one of the greatest ways to craft a book that would give your readers real value for their money. *Research about facts, events, stories, trends, phenomena, statistics, and discoveries that people can relate with.* This more than any other thing would add color to your content and make it more captivating for your readers. Another important time to research is when you run out of ideas or encounter what is known as a writer's block. At such moments take a break, look for inspiration around you, in people's words, or anything else. The moment you get that spark of inspiration or a fresh insight into what you are writing about, get back to work!

STEP 13

AVOID PLAGIARISM

This is the act of copying another author's text without acknowledging them for the information or mentioning their name to give them credit for their work. This is a literary offence and is capable of "de-branding" you as an author. It could also lead to a lawsuit that can cost you lots of money. If you must copy a text word for word, then you should reference the author as the original source of that information. In such cases you should mention the name of the author of that text and the title of the book or article you are referring to. Even when you are not copying verbatim, you should reference the sources of your information in the book. This can be done after the last chapter of your book. It gives your book a professional outlook and makes people see your work as authentic. However, when you fail to do proper referencing, you present yourself as an amateur and a literary thief.

STEP 14

ADD YOUR CONTACT DETAILS

Remember that your book is also a marketing tool for your brand. Make sure you have a contact phone number and email through which you can be reached by your readers or by a potential client. I have received several business deals from people who read my books and decided to get in touch with me because they loved my work. That has brought me several speaking gigs and more business opportunities. You can have your contact details and/or social media handles at the front where the copyright and ISBN details can be located. It could also be on the concluding pages of your book or on both if you deem it necessary.

STEP 15

ADD A CAPTIVATING AUTHOR BIO

You need a short and precise description of yourself. This can be used to establish your image and project your brand as a credible and a good one. Before people buy the book of an author, they are not familiar with, they would normally glance through to check the author bio. They do this so they can have an idea of the author's personality and justify their buying decision and reading choice. Take advantage of that and always draft a great author bio for each book you write.

STEP 16

ADD A COMPELLING BOOK BLURB

This is a short but captivating description of what your book is about and why your potential reader needs to get it immediately. Most authors take this for granted without knowing its importance. Make sure you take your time to craft a great but precise book description or blurb. It matters a lot because people always want to have a summary of a book to decide if it is worth reading. Also, the attention span of the average individual is very low, and so, only a captivating book description can give them a reason to stay disciplined till they complete your book. Therefore, your book description must effectively communicate the benefits a potential reader stands to get from your book.

STEP 17

GET SOMEONE TO CRITIQUE YOUR WORK

It is very helpful to get someone credible to read through your work to see if you have a content that could wow the readers it was designed for. This approach can be helpful especially for a first-time author. It has a way of helping the author ascertain whether the book he is about to publish is well put together. This person should be someone who would critically examine your ideas and perspectives on the subject matter you wrote about. It should not be someone who would rundown your work and efforts with discouraging remarks and bias judgment. Some people are so negative that when you give them the opportunity to critique your work, they destroy the beauty of what you have written and say all kinds of negative things that could discourage you. You don't want to give such a person your book to examine or scrutinize either. It should be someone that can tell you the truth and give you honest feedback in a way that inspires you to do more. Such individuals are also expected not to steal your intellectual property hence they should be trustworthy persons who would not compromise your brainchild

STEP 18

GET SOMEONE COMPETENT TO PROOFREAD YOUR WORK

This is a very important phase of the book completion process. There is a difference between critiquing and proofreading. While former means evaluating and reviewing the ideas and concepts contained in your book, the later looks to examine the grammatical correctness of your work. Poor editing can be the difference between a wonderful book and a terrible book. You should get someone proficient in the use of English or whatever language you have chosen to proof-read your work, to check for spelling errors, grammatical errors, and typo errors. This is the role an editor plays as they help eliminate any language blunders that may arise in your manuscript. They can also make suggestions on how best you can present your ideas and structure your work if possible. There are many freelance editors on www.fiverr.com and www.upwork.com. You can use them if you have checked their profile to know how credible and effective, they are. You can also use the help of learned friends, colleagues, or mentors if they are capable and would be willing to make out time to help you. Ultimately, you can do it yourself if you have the capacity and time, and you do not have competent people who can do it for you, but I wouldn't recommend that.

CONCLUSION

Congratulations!!! I'm so glad you made it this far. Now you have the framework you need to start, develop, and complete your book without abandoning it. That brainchild of yours is almost ready to be birthed into the world where it was destined to find expression, make impact, transform lives, solve problems, and bring you fulfilment along with all the trappings of success.

Now that you have what it takes to complete your book manuscript, we can get into deeper and more intimate discussions pertaining to packaging, publishing, launching, selling, marketing, and scaling your book idea into a book brand and business. If at this point you are not receiving emails from me, now would be the best time to sign up for more content. I would be sending tips and updates that would help you take your journey to the next level.

Feel free to provide some feedback or reviews on this book you have just read. Tag me on social media @iredafeowolabi, use hashtag #stepstowriteyourbook and rave about this content for others who may need this to also hear the word. You can send your feedback or request to join my newsletter where I share valuable content to subscribers on how to succeed as an author. Send these to writeyourbook@iredafeowolabi.com .

www.ingramcontent.com/pod-product-compliance
Lightning Source LLC
Chambersburg PA
CBHW051123250726
48655CB00007B/2861